ANIMALS AT WORK

Animals Caring for Their Young

WORLD BOOK

World Book, Inc.
180 North LaSalle Street
Suite 900
Chicago, Illinois 60601
USA

Produced for World Book, Inc. by Bailey Publishing Associates Ltd.

For information about other World Book publications, visit our website at **www.worldbook.com** or call **1-800-WORLDBK (967-5325).**

Library of Congress Cataloging-in-Publication data has been applied for.

Title: Animals Caring for Their Young
ISBN: 978-0-7166-2726-5

Animals at Work
ISBN: 978-0-7166-2724-1 (set, hc)

Also available as:
ISBN: 978-0-7166-2739-5 (e-book)

Printed in China by Shenzhen Wing King Tong
Paper Products Co, Ltd., Shenzhen, Guangdong
1st printing August 2018

Staff

Writer: Cath Senker

Executive Committee

President
Jim O'Rourke

Vice President and Editor in Chief
Paul A. Kobasa

Vice President, Finance
Donald D. Keller

Vice President, Marketing
Jean Lin

Vice President, International
Maksim Rutenberg

Vice President, Technology
Jason Dole

Director, Human Resources
Bev Ecker

Editorial

Director, Print Publishing
Tom Evans

Managing Editor
Jeff De La Rosa

Editor
William D. Adams

Manager, Contracts & Compliance
(Rights & Permissions)
Loranne K. Shields

Manager, Indexing Services
David Pofelski

Librarian
S. Thomas Richardson

Digital

Director, Digital Product
Development
Erika Meller

Digital Product Manager
Jonathan Wills

Manufacturing/Production

Manufacturing Manager
Anne Fritzinger

Proofreader
Nathalie Strassheim

Graphics and Design

Senior Art Director
Tom Evans

Senior Designer
Don Di Sante

Media Editor
Rosalia Bledsoe

Special thanks to:

Roberta Bailey
Nicola Barber
Francis Paola Lea
Claire Munday
Alex Woolf

Acknowledgments

Cover photo: © Alizada Studios/Shutterstock

Alamy: 8, 12, 20 & 30 (blickwinkel), 8-9 (Susan & Allan Parker), 9 (Keith Douglas), 11 (Skip Higgins of Raskal Photography), 14 (All Canada Photos), 16 (James Schwabel), 17 (S. Biesmans - Wild Life Projects), 18-19 (Michael Patrick O'Neill), 23 (Doug Perrine), 24 (Ivan Kuzmin), 24-25 (Konrad Wothe/Minden Pictures), 26 (Steve Bloom Images), 29 (Minden Pictures), 42 (Florian Schulz), 43 (Arco Images GmbH), 45 (dbimages). **Jorge Almeida**: 30-31. **Shutterstock**: title page & 38-9 (Artush), 4 (Sergey Uryadnikov), 5 (Craig Fraser), 6 (Toni Patzke), 6-7 (Brett Hondow), 10 (Natalia Kuzmina), 10-11 (Stacey Ann Alberts), 12-13 (mnoor), 14-15 (dioch), 16-17 (Mark Medcalf), 18 (reptiles4all), 20-21 (mj - tim photography), 26-27 (Zuzana Gabrielova), 33 (Studio 37), 34-35 (Alta Oosthuizen), 35 (George Lamson), 36-37 (Lehrer), 40-41 (Gudkov Andrey), 41 (sirtravelalot), 42-43 (Ondrej Prosicky).

A mother koala carries her young on her back in Australia. A young koala spends the first year of its life with its mother, growing in her pouch and riding on her back.

Contents

Introduction

Animals vary in shape and size, but all animal **species** depend on offspring (young) for survival. Having offspring enables a species to grow and spread. Offspring also replace individuals killed by **predators,** disease, age, or other causes. Without offspring to keep up its numbers, an animal species would quickly become **extinct.**

Simple animals, including sponges, corals, and hydra, make offspring on their own. The hydra, for example, a tiny creature that lives in lakes and ponds, simply grows a new hydra on its side. The little one breaks off to become a new individual.

But most animals make offspring through sexual **reproduction.** In sexual reproduction, the **sperm** from a male **fertilizes** the female's **eggs.** Many animals lay their eggs. Others keep their eggs inside the body, where they grow and develop into young that are born live. All birds lay eggs, as do most fish, **amphibians,** and **reptiles.** Virtually all **mammals,** and some reptiles and fish, give birth to live young.

When they are ready to hatch, chicks push through the egg wall with the tips of their beaks.

Making offspring is not enough, though, to ensure the survival of a species. To contribute to the future of the species, the offspring must themselves survive. Animal parents can help their young to survive by providing care. The amount and kind of care animals give their offspring varies. Many animals deposit a pile of eggs and immediately abandon them. But some animals carry their young in their bodies for many months, provide food for them after they are born, and watch over them for many years until they are ready to strike out on their own.

In this book, we describe the different methods animals use to care for their young, from the animals that provide the least care to those that work the hardest. We focus on parents that go the extra mile to make sure their young survive.

Parental investment

An animal taking care of its young is using time and energy that could be spent in other ways. It could instead be finding food for itself, looking for more chances to **mate,** or protecting itself more carefully from predators. The amount of resources an animal spends on its offspring is known as *parental investment.* Many animals carefully balance the amount of time and energy they spend on one group of offspring with their chances to mate again. Other animals reproduce only once, and so may do everything they can to ensure their **brood** survives.

Giraffes take good care of their young.

You're on Your Own

Some animals provide no care to their offspring. Females lay hundreds, thousands, or even millions of **eggs** at a time, but then both parents abandon them. Instead, the parents look out for themselves and prepare for the next **mating.**

MILLIONS OF EGGS

Most fish, such as cod, use this strategy. Females lay millions of eggs, which the males **fertilize.** The eggs are then scattered in the open water. Almost all of the eggs become meals for other animals—some fish even eat their own eggs. When the survivors hatch, they are tiny and face many **predators.** Out of thousands or millions, only a few eggs grow into adult fish.

A TADPOLE-EAT-TADPOLE WORLD

Most frogs lay large clumps of eggs in water and abandon them. The eggs hatch into tiny tadpoles. Left unprotected, most of the eggs and tadpoles become meals for other animals. Some tadpoles even eat other tadpoles! They have large mouths and will hunt down and eat the tadpoles of other frogs. In other **species,** tadpoles will eat their brothers and sisters if food is in short supply. Out of hundreds of fertilized eggs, only a few live to become frogs.

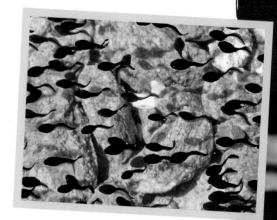

Only a few of these tadpoles will survie long enough to turn into frogs.

Why abandon one's young?

Why do many animals abandon their offspring without so much as a second thought? Being a good parent takes many resources and can be quite dangerous. By looking out for themselves, the parents are increasing the chances that they will be able to **reproduce** again. Only a very small number of their offspring might survive, but it will be enough to keep the **species** going.

A ladybug lays up to 50 eggs at a time.

PICKING THE RIGHT SPOT

For many animals, parental care consists of picking just the right spot to lay their **eggs.** Doing so might ensure that the eggs are protected from the weather or **predators,** or that there will be a good meal waiting for the young when they hatch. Picking a good site for laying eggs can make all the difference to the hatchlings' survival.

Butterfly mothers often set their offspring up for success by laying their eggs on a favorite type of plant. A female may lay up to 300 tiny eggs on the plant and then fly away. When the eggs hatch, the hungry caterpillars—the **larval** stage of a butterfly—have a handy food supply.

Most spider **species** protect their eggs by wrapping them in a silken egg sac. This helps keep the eggs safe and warm. Even after they hatch, the spiderlings of most species stay in the egg sac while their bodies continue to grow. If the eggs are laid in autumn, the spiderlings stay inside the egg sac until spring brings warmer weather.

BROOD PARASITES

For some birds, fish, and **insects,** the best spot for a female to lay its eggs is in the nest of a different species. These **brood parasites** use **mimicry** to trick—or even bullying, to force—the **host** parents into caring for their babies. Brood parasites include the brown-headed cowbird, cuckoo bee, and the cuckoo catfish. The European cuckoo lays its eggs in the nests of smaller birds. When the cuckoo chick hatches, it shoves any other eggs and young out of the nest. The foster parents accept the intruder, raising the cuckoo as their own.

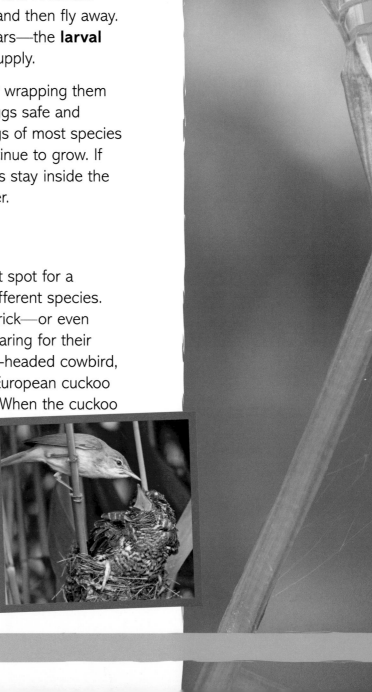

A reed warbler feeds the cuckoo chick that has taken over its nest.

The female nursery web spider spins a silk tent to protect her spiderlings as they hatch.

Sticky eggs

Herring are fish that live in the waters along seacoasts of the North Atlantic and North Pacific oceans. A female herring lays about 40,000 eggs, mostly on plants, seaweed, or rocks. The eggs are sticky, so they fix onto the surface where they are laid. Atlantic herring may lay their eggs on the ocean bed. There, they have some defense against predators and cannot drift away to areas with poor conditions for hatching.

Sticky herring eggs cover this seaweed.

Nest Is Best

Even when female animals take care in laying their **eggs,** all kinds of things can harm the eggs or young. Some animals improve their care by building a nest. Such nests are often fiercely guarded by the parents, allowing many of their offspring to reach adulthood. Some animals go to great lengths to build safe nurseries for their offspring.

BIRDS

Birds build nests in all shapes and sizes. The most common are shaped like a bowl or saucer, perfect for holding eggs. Birds build them in holes in the ground or in bushes or trees for protection. They use the materials they find around them—twigs, grass, and leaves. Different **species** make their nests in different places, depending on their **habitat.** Woodpeckers build their nests inside trees, while kingfishers dig theirs in sand or clay banks. Some swallows nest on the side of cliffs at the coast or in caves. Buildings make useful nesting places, too. House sparrows and pigeons form nests under the eaves of houses.

Some birds build elaborate nests to protect their young from **predators** and bad weather. Weaver birds make baskets of woven grass and plant fibers, making sure they are completely enclosed, except for a small opening. The nest hangs from tree branches or reeds. The eggs are kept inside, and only the parents can go in and out. The tailorbird sews the edges of one or two large leaves together, using grass, and hides its nest inside. These well-built homes give the young a good start in life.

The American cliff swallow builds its nest out of mud.

A male Southern masked weaver checks on his woven nest.

A tree nest is a safe place for this gray squirrel and its young.

Not just for baby

For some animals, nests are important for the survival of adults as well as their offspring. Squirrels use nests not only to raise their young, but to stay warm in the winter and cool in the summer, hide from predators, and store food. A squirrel usually has more than one nest and can quickly move to another if threatened.

OTHER NEST BUILDERS

Although birds are the most familiar nest-builders, many kinds of animals make structures to protect their offspring. Salmon and trout are fish that dig simple gravel nests in which to lay their **eggs.** Once the eggs have been laid and **fertilized,** the fish cover them with more gravel to hide them from **predators** and protect them from strong water currents, which might wash them away. Male Siamese fightingfish blow bubbles that stick together to make a nest. After **mating,** the male collects the eggs in his mouth and blows them into the nest. The bubbles keep the eggs together and help them to get enough oxygen. The male guards the nest until the eggs hatch.

The duck-billed platypus—a type of animal called a **monotreme**—of Australia also builds a nest. Unlike most **mammals,** which give birth to live young, the platypus lays eggs. It builds a nest of leaves and grass at the end of its burrow, dug into the banks of streams. The young stay in the nest, fed by their mother's milk, until they are about four months old.

The burying beetle makes a nest with its young's food source. Both the male and female find the **carcass** of a small animal, such as a rat or a bird. They move it to suitable ground, remove all of its feathers or fur, and bury it. The parents cover the carcass in substances to stop it rotting and create a dent on top of the carcass. The female lays the eggs in a side chamber of the nest. When the eggs hatch, the parents place the **larvae** into the dent. The parents slowly eat the carcass and **regurgitate** the food for the larvae. At the start, the larvae depend on their parents to deliver them regurgitated food, even begging just as bird nestlings do.

The burying beetle does an important job in getting rid of dead animals.

A Siamese fightingfish guards newly laid eggs in a bubble nest.

INCUBATION

In the nest, **eggs** need proper conditions to develop. Often they need to be at temperatures warmer than the outside air. Parents work hard to keep their eggs under proper conditions for growth and development. This is called **incubation.** Most birds sit on their eggs to incubate them. In many **species,** the female incubates the eggs. In other species, both parents take their turn. In a few species, including shorebirds called phalaropes (*FAL uh rohps),* incubation is the male's job.

In most cases, the birds doing the incubating have a bare area of skin on their body called a brood patch. This patch is full of blood vessels, helping the bird to more efficiently transfer heat from its body to the eggs.

As it stretches, this chinstrap penguin reveals the brood patch on its belly.

Other animals use their body heat to warm eggs. A female python winds herself around her eggs to guard them and provide warmth, so the snake **embryos** develop more quickly. Despite being a **cold-blooded** animal, she can raise her own body temperature to heat the eggs.

Some animals have found another incubation solution. In most species of crocodiles, females lay up to 80 eggs and bury them in riverbanks, where the mothers defend them from **predators.** The sun heats the ground and keeps the eggs at a constant temperature. In shady **habitats,** crocodiles may cover their eggs with rotting plants to warm them. At hatching time, the babies call out from inside their eggs, and mom digs them up. Using a spike on their snout, the babies crack their way out of the shell. The mother gives them a ride in her mouth to the water to feed. Megapodes, turkey-like birds living in Australasia, bury their eggs in large mounds of soil and rotting plants. The decaying (breaking down) of the plants gives off heat that warms the eggs.

Baby crocodiles are born with sharp teeth, ready for hunting.

GUARDING THE NEST

Parents invest a huge amount of energy in making offspring and building a nest. Most will ferociously guard their young against **predators** and rivals. Almost all birds will aggressively defend their nests with swoops, pecks, and scratches when a predator comes close. Male freshwater bass guard their **eggs** and will fiercely attack any invaders. The female king cobra snake coils above her nest for about two months to protect the 20 to 50 eggs within. Octopus mothers also watch closely over their eggs. One octopus was seen to guard her eggs for four and a half years, eating little or nothing the whole time. When the young hatched, the mother died.

Some parents will even guard their young for a time after they have left the nest. Among fish, freshwater bass, bowfin, brown bullhead catfish, and some stickleback fathers watch over their young for a while. Like crocodiles (see pages 14-15), alligators guard the nest and take their hatchlings to the water. The babies form social groups called pods for protection, but the mother is on hand, too. If the young are in danger, they call her. Alligator mothers watch over their offspring for a year or more. By this time, they have new babies to look after.

A mother alligator watches over her young in Everglades National Park, Florida.

An Arctic tern defends
its nest with swoops
and fierce cries.

The gladiator tree frog

In the tropical Central American country of Costa
Rica, gladiator tree frogs come down from the
trees to marshy areas in the breeding season.
The male builds a nest, which fills with water.
After **mating,** the female lays her eggs there.
The male defends the nest from rival males that
would destroy his **brood.** If he hears an outsider,
the gladiator tree frog makes lots of noise,
hissing, barking, and growling. If the enemy is
not put off, the defending frog will chase him
away or fight.

When defending
their nests, male
gladiator tree frogs
are vicious fighters.

Hitching a Ride

Rather than build and guard nests, some animals take their **eggs** or young along with them. This allows the parents to protect and care for their offspring while going about their usual routine.

A MOUTH NEST

Male sea catfishes and some other fish **species** carry eggs in their mouths. The eggs are less likely to be eaten by **predators** there than in the open water or in nests. The hardhead sea catfish holds the **fertilized** eggs in his mouth for up to 80 days. For two weeks after they hatch, the tiny **fry** swim back into their father's mouth for protection if they sense danger.

The male Darwin's frog from South America picks up his **mate's** eggs when they are about to hatch and carries them around in his vocal pouch, a sac on his neck that expands to hold the **brood.** The vocal pouch is home to the young until they are ready to live on their own. Once they have become froglets, they hop out of his mouth!

SPIDER CARETAKERS

Some species of spiders and their relatives protect their offspring before and after they are born. After fertilization, the female wolf spider protects the eggs in a silken egg sac attached to the end of her body. After the baby spiders hatch, the female opens the egg sac. The spiderlings crawl out onto the female's back, where they cling to special hairs. The spiderlings ride on the mother's back for about a week or more as they grow.

Wolf spiderlings hitch a ride on their mother's back.

The male banded jawfish incubates his mate's eggs in his mouth.

Why is there a larval stage?

The fertilized eggs of **amphibians** do not contain enough **nutrients** for the young to develop completely. Instead, they hatch as **larvae.** The larvae feed hungrily and grow quickly so they can turn into adults.

BABY IN A POUCH

Some kinds of **mammals** carry their young in a pouch. They are called **marsupials.** Marsupials include kangaroos, koalas, and opossums. About two-thirds of them live in Australia and nearby islands.

A kangaroo joey (baby) develops for just 33 days inside its mother—a brief time compared to an average of 340 days for a horse, for example. It is not surprising that the joey is so small at birth. It is just 1 inch (2.5 centimeters) long—smaller than a finger—and has no back legs. It uses its more developed front legs to climb to the pouch. There, it searches for a teat to **suckle** milk. The baby stays feeding and sleeping in the pouch for 70 days. Then it starts to move around in there.

Another marsupial, the Tasmanian devil, gives birth to up to 50 pups, but has only four teats in her pouch. Once born, the tiny pups race to get to a teat. The four winners stay feeding in their mother's pouch for three months. The rest die within a few hours.

STUCK ON YOU

Some **species** of **amphibians** attach their **eggs** directly to their body. The female midwife toad lays from 20 to 60 eggs in two strings. Her **mate** fastens them to his legs and carries them until they hatch. He usually hides on land beneath a stone or underground while he carries the eggs. He comes out after dark and bathes the eggs in a pond or stream. After three weeks, he takes the eggs into the water, and tadpoles hatch from them.

After a pair of Surinam toads mate, the male sweeps the eggs on to the back of the female. They stick to her back and get under her skin. Here they develop, without a tadpole stage. Around two and a half months later, they hatch as little toadlets and come out from their mother's skin. With this protection, most eggs turn into toads.

The male midwife toad takes care of the eggs until they hatch.

Spot the joey peeking out of its mother's pouch.

A CLOSER LOOK
Dads
Giving Birth

The seahorse is a strange-looking little fish with a long, tubelike snout and prehensile (grasping) tail. It lives mostly in shallow tropical oceans. Male seahorses are the only male animals that give birth to live young. The female's body swells with up to several hundred **eggs.** Using an egg duct—a sort of pipe for depositing eggs—she places them in a brood pouch at the base of the male's tail. The male **fertilizes** the eggs and keeps them in his pouch.

The male is in charge of caring for the eggs. His body supplies oxygen and **nutrients.** He is able to adjust the salt levels in his pouch, which gradually change from the levels in his body to that of the salt water outside. This helps the babies to be ready for life in the ocean when they are born. The eggs hatch into young called sea foals while still in the father's brood pouch, and they remain inside to continue development. Depending on the **species,** the male carries the young for 10 to 45 days.

When it is time for the sea foals to be born, the seahorse's body shakes violently, and he pushes out the young through an opening in his pouch. The foals float together in groups, holding on to each other's tails. At this point, childcare ends and the babies must take care of themselves. The male gets another batch of eggs from his partner, and the life cycle continues.

A MALE SEAHORSE expels fry from its brood pouch.

In some seahorse species, the same pair produces many **broods** during the breeding season. They have huge numbers of young because fewer than five baby seahorses out of 1,000 live to become adults. Yet because the father shelters the eggs while they develop, seahorse babies survive at a higher rate than the babies of many other fish.

Feeding Baby

Some parents give their young food. The parents may give the young some of what they eat, find special food for them to eat, or even make food for the young.

SHARING PARENTS

For many parent animals, the easiest option is to feed their offspring whatever they eat. In some kinds of spiders, the spiderlings hatch from the **egg** sac and live in their mother's web for a while, sharing her food. Wolves live in packs and bring up their cubs together. Adult wolves hunt and come back to the den with meat, which they **regurgitate** for the youngsters. When they are a few months old, the cubs learn to hunt with the adults. Coyotes and African hunting dogs also bring meat to the family.

SCORPION

Scorpion eggs hatch inside the female a few days after she **mates** with a male. The babies stay in the mother's **ovary,** feeding on a milk-like substance that comes through the mother's stomach wall. They live there for several weeks as they grow into scorplings. The little scorplings have pincers and stingers but they are too small and soft to survive on their own. They hitch a ride on their mother's back and eat bits of the food she catches. When they have developed a tough exoskeleton (hard outer shell), they are ready to leave.

Scorplings live on their mother's back for about a month.

Two gray wolf pups beg for food from their mother.

Special diet

Sometimes, an animal may collect a special food for its young to eat. Such food may be full of **nutrients** to help the young animals grow quickly. For instance, sparrows feed their chicks a diet of **insects** for the 8 to 10 days they spend in the nest. The high-protein diet helps the chicks develop. When the young leave the nest, they switch to their grown-up diet of seeds and grain.

MOTHER'S MILK

All **mammals** feed on their mother's milk. In this way, mammal mothers can take good care of their offspring and make sure that many survive into adulthood. Most mammals suck milk from their mother's nipples. In **monotremes,** such as the duck-billed platypus (see page 12), milk is released through pores (tiny holes) on the stomach, and the young lap it up.

The hooded seal, which lives in the Arctic, has the shortest nursing period of any mammal. Most of the pups are **weaned** just four days after they are born! But most mammals nurse for weeks or months. Some, including elephants and rhinos, nurse their young for several years. The young continue to drink the milk even after they start to eat solid food.

Whales feed their young highly concentrated (thick and rich) milk. It is far richer in fat, protein, and minerals than the milk of land mammals. This rich food helps whale calves to grow quickly. For example, baby blue whales gain about 200 pounds (90 kilograms) per day.

CROP MILK

Emperor penguins, flamingos, and pigeons are birds that make a kind of food for their young. They feed their babies with a **nutrient**-rich substance made in their crop (a baglike area near the throat). The substance they produce is "crop milk," and it contains lots of fat and protein. Flamingos feed their chicks on crop milk for about two weeks. Then, the chicks gather in a group called a crèche (*krehsh, kraysh)* and begin to find their own food, filtering tiny living things from the water themselves.

Both male and female flamingos can make crop milk.

Emperor penguins use crop milk as an emergency food source. Couples breed during the Antarctic winter, and the female leaves the **egg** with the male while she walks to the ocean to eat. After four months, the egg hatches, around the same time that the mother comes back from feeding. But if the mother is late, the father will give the chick crop milk. When the mother comes back, the parents take turns going to the ocean, feeding their chick with **regurgitated** fish.

An impala calf suckles milk from its mother.

Strawberry Poison Dart Frog

Living in the rain forests of Central America, strawberry poison dart frogs are dedicated parents. The female lays her **eggs** on a leaf on the rain forest floor. Then the male takes up his duties. To keep the eggs moist until they hatch, he urinates (*YUR uh nayts;* gets rid of liquid waste) on them. He checks that they are healthy, and eats any that are infected with **fungi** or that do not develop, as well as eggs left by other males.

After a week, the eggs hatch into tadpoles, and the mother comes back. She carries each baby one at a time on her back and climbs up a tree. The frog mother has to house her tadpoles separately, because if they remain together, they will eat each other. She carefully picks a plant, often one that grows on the limbs of trees. The plant is sometimes high up in the tops of the trees, a long way from the frog's **habitat** on the ground. She searches for a cup-shaped leaf containing a pool of water to be her tadpole's own little nursery. The tadpole itself chooses the exact spot! It vibrates when mom finds a good place. It is harder for **predators** to reach the tadpole here than on the rain forest floor, so it is more likely to survive.

In their treetop nurseries, the tadpoles have to be fed. To stay alive, the tadpole needs a meal within three days of its arrival in its nursery. The mother frog visits each baby and lays an unfertilized egg in the pool, the only food the young can eat. She comes back every few days to feed her tadpoles until they grow into frogs—which means many trips up and down trees. Meanwhile, the father guards the area to stop other frogs from finding and eating the babies. Within six to eight weeks, the tadpoles turn into froglets and come out of their nurseries.

A STRAWBERRY POISON DART FROG female makes the long journey up from the rain forest floor with a tadpole on her back

PIECES OF YOU

Some animal mothers feed their young with pieces of themselves. Caecilians are legless **amphibians** that look a lot like snakes. They live in rain forests. Some **species** lay **eggs,** while many give birth to live young. Most egg-laying caecilians guard their eggs until they hatch and then leave them. Taita African caecilians from the east-central African country of Kenya are different. Their babies are born helpless and dependent on their mother. She has an amazing way of feeding the hatchlings—with her own skin! The top layer of mom's skin becomes rich in protein and fat, and her babies have sharp teeth for tearing off and chewing it. The mother's skin regrows every three days. Yet she loses about one-seventh of her body weight while feeding her young. It is her sacrifice to help the survival of the next generation.

Some mother spiders die so their young will live. When the young of one of these spider mothers are ready to feed, she allows herself to become their first meal. Different species give themselves up in different ways. In *Stegodyphus lineatus* (*steh goh DY fuhs lihn ee AH tuhs),* a spider of the Negev Desert in the Middle Eastern country of Israel, the mother turns most of her insides into a liquid and **regurgitates** it out of her mouth for her young to lap up. When the spiderlings have grown strong enough to feed on their own, they eat what is left of the mother spider with their piercing mouthparts. The nutrition offered from the mother's body will help the spiderlings reach adulthood and make their own spiderlings.

The Taita African caecilian lives in a small area of the Taita Hills in Kenya.

Maternal investment

Female animals invest a lot of resources into their young. Eggs are large and full of **nutrients** to allow the **embryos** to develop, so females usually spend a large portion of their gathered resources on the offspring even before they are born. On the other hand, **sperm** requires fewer resources to create. This may explain why, among animals, females are more likely to care for their offspring than males.

These spiderlings are feeding off their mother's dead body.

A CLOSER LOOK
Helping Hatchlings

Discus fish are colorful tropical fish from the Amazon. They raise their young with **mammal**-like care, protecting them until they can take care of themselves. Both the mother and father take part in parenting.

After the **eggs** hatch, the baby fish stay attached to the surface where the eggs were laid and absorb the egg yolk for food. Once they can all swim on their own, they leave the surface as a group. The parents make a **mucus** that covers their own bodies, and the baby fish feed on it until they are able to find food themselves. The **fry** nibble at the side of mom for about 10 minutes. Then she pushes them over to dad to take over feeding duties. The parents feed their babies in this way for two weeks, providing constant care.

The protein and **antibodies** in discus fish mucus increase when the eggs are laid. The young need protein for growth and antibodies for protection from disease. Protein and antibody levels stay high until the third week, when the fry begin to find their own food.

BABY DISCUS FISH feed off their parents' mucus until they are old enough to take care of themselves.

Once the babies are three weeks old, the parents start to swim away from them for short periods. This encourages the fry to learn to be on their own. The babies feed less from their parents' mucus and start to look for food themselves. By the fourth week, the fry barely feed off their parents at all. They are now independent and ready to begin life alone.

Group Parenting

Parenting is hard work. In some animals, it takes more than just one pair of parents to raise the young. Spreading around the responsibility and work helps the young get the best care possible.

MEERKAT COMMUNITY CARE

Meerkats are small burrowing **mammals** that live in the semi-deserts of southern Africa. They live and raise their young in a community. They dig their dens underground, where they are protected from **predators.** Survival in the harsh, dry **habitat** is tough, so meerkats use teamwork. Most of them search for food, some watch out for danger, and others care for the kits—the young.

Kits are born in the safety of the den. During the first few weeks, while most of the adults leave to search for food, one meerkat guards the kits, defending them from attack by other meerkat groups. The guard warns them if danger appears from land or air. When they are about a month old, the kits join the pack outside the den. Female helpers carry them if they fall behind and feed them milk. The helpers nurse the kits even if they are not their mothers. As the kits grow, adults teach them to hunt **prey.** At first, they bring the kits dead scorpions. As the kits learn, adults bring them live scorpions to toy with, but they bite the dangerous scorpion stingers off. By three months old, the kits have learned to catch scorpions by themselves.

Meerkats on the lookout for danger near their den.

Sea lion nurseries

Galápagos sea lions live on the Galápagos Islands about 600 miles (1,000 kilometers) off the coast of Ecuador, in South America. Groups of up to 30 female sea lions give birth on a beach, guarded by a male. Once the babies are a week old, the mothers drop them off at a rookery—a sea-lion nursery where pups feed, play, and nap together. Female caretakers, who often have their own young, take turns looking after the pups while the other females enter the water to feed.

A Galápagos sea lion pup may be watched by other females while its mother hunts for food.

RAISING BABY ANTS

In ant **colonies,** all the members of the community are related. The queen is the mother and lays all the **eggs.** The eggs develop into **larvae, pupae,** and then into adults.

The first eggs to hatch become the worker ants, and the queen feeds them with her saliva and with eggs. The workers bring in food from outside the nest, so the queen can focus on egg laying. Larvae that will become soldiers, males, and winged females hatch from later batches of eggs. Worker "nurses" feed them solid food. These nurse ants eat a sweet liquid made by the larvae.

As they grow, the larvae shed their skin several times. After a few weeks, they become pupae. They spin a **cocoon** around themselves. The cocoon is made out of a sort of thin thread the larvae make. Inside they change into adults. When the ant is ready to break out, the nurse ant bites a hole in the cocoon and helps the youngster to climb out. The nurse washes and feeds the young ant. Now it is ready for its adult duties.

BEE BABY CARE

Like ants, honey bees and bumble bees are **insects** that live together and cooperate to build colonies and raise their young. Only the queen has babies. The workers are her children and help to bring up the next generation.

A honey bee queen lays her eggs in the cells of a honeycomb. Three days later, the eggs hatch into larvae. The workers are in charge of baby care. They feed the larvae with a rich, creamy substance called royal jelly, produced by the worker bees. After three days, the workers switch to feeding most of the larvae with beebread, made from pollen and honey. The workers select just a few larvae as future queens, and they continue to feed them with royal jelly.

By five days old, a larva has fed on enough beebread to grow into the size of an adult bee and fill its cell. A worker covers the cell with wax, and the larva spins a cocoon and turns into a pupa. About 16 days later, it has developed into a winged adult worker and is ready to come out. The new member of the colony gets to work.

Queen of the ants

The queen is far bigger than all the other ants. In one **species,** she is 1,000 times larger than the workers! She spends virtually her whole life laying eggs. Queen ants leave caring for the larvae and baby ants to the larvae's older sisters.

Worker bees take care of the larvae in the cells of the honeycomb.

A Female Society

Elephant society is run by its females. Cows (adult female elephants) and calves (babies) live in family groups, led by the oldest female. The males leave when they become adults—at around 12 for African and 14 for Asian elephants—and just visit the family occasionally. Yet females stay with their mother until she dies.

A baby elephant is born after 18 to 22 months inside its mother, the longest time of any **mammal.** Around 3 feet tall (1 meter) tall and weighing about 220 pounds (100 kilograms), the calf can walk less than an hour after birth, although it is a little wobbly at first. It stays close to its mother for its first three months to **suckle** milk—with its mouth, not its trunk.

Other females help to care for the calf, usually young elephants that have not yet had their own babies. These babysitters are learning to be good parents. All members of the group are affectionate toward the youngsters, and older elephants adjust their pace of walking so the little one can keep up. If there is danger from other animals, the elephants make a circle, with the calf protected in the middle.

At three to four months, the infant starts grazing on plants, and by the age of one, it can run around and feed itself. Yet it stays

close to its mother and continues to nurse for another year or two. Often it only stops nursing when mom becomes tired of being poked by the calf's growing tusks. The calf gets plenty of attention because its mother will not have another calf before the youngster is four.

Elephants are caring creatures. The more females there are to look after a calf, the more likely it is to survive. Elephants show friendship toward each other and sadness when a family member dies. Mothers show great sadness if a baby is stillborn—born dead.

An AFRICAN ELEPHANT with its baby drinking at a waterhole in Hwange National Park, Zimbabwe.

Hard-Working Moms (and Dads)

Sometimes, a single parent works extremely hard to raise and protect its offspring. Usually, the lone parent is a mother, but in some **species,** fathers take on all the responsibility.

POLAR BEARS

A mother polar bear digs her den in the snow. In December or January, she gives birth to one or two tiny cubs, weighing only about 1.5 pounds (0.68 kilogram) each. She nurses her babies but cannot feed herself. In late March or April, the mother and cubs come out of the den. By then the mother is hungry and thin—she has not eaten for five months. She breaks into the dens of ringed seals, hunting seal babies. Mostly she fails—only 1 in 20 hunts is successful. If she fails to catch a seal quickly, her milk dries up and the cubs die. Surviving cubs stay with their mother until they are two-and-a-half years old. She feeds them and protects them from attack by adult males.

CHEETAHS

A cheetah mother usually has three to five cubs, which she cares for in her den. Raising the cubs alone is difficult. After a couple of days, the den starts to smell of cheetah. Lions or hyenas may catch the scent and attack the cubs—many baby cheetahs are killed in their first three months. The best way to protect the cubs is to move them regularly. Mom switches to a new den every four days, carrying her babies one by one to their next temporary home. The cubs live with mom for up to 18 months, while she teaches them how to hunt. When the cubs leave their mother, they all stay together for six months, until they are ready to live on their own.

Why do cubs play?

Polar bear cubs watch their mom hunt and copy her moves. When they tumble around together having mock fights, they are developing their muscles and coordination to practice their hunting skills.

Polar bear cubs love to play in the snow.

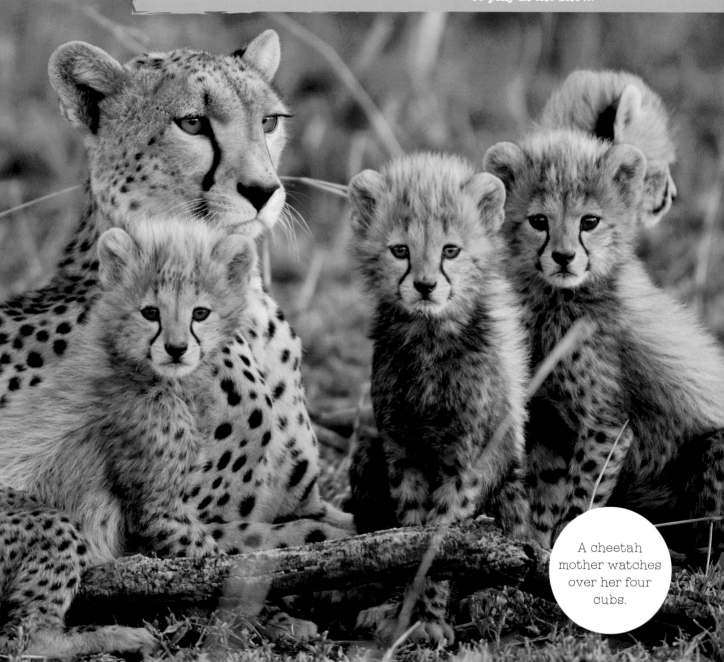

A cheetah mother watches over her four cubs.

LONE DADS AND CO-PARENTS

For most birds, raising young is the job of both parents, but some male birds take on the task alone. The rhea is a large, flightless bird from South America. The male **mates** with many females, then he builds a shallow nest on the ground, lines it with grass, and brings several hens to lay their **eggs.** There may be up to 30 eggs in his nest. The hens' job is done, and they go off to mate with other males. The father **incubates** the eggs until they hatch six weeks later. He cares for the young for another six weeks, defending them aggressively against any animal that comes near.

Spotted sandpiper father birds are generally in charge of childcare, too. The female mates with up to four males. She leaves four eggs with each one before going off to seek another mate. Each male incubates the eggs. Once they have hatched, he looks after the babies for at least four weeks while they learn to fly. Sometimes, the female helps out. After leaving eggs with various partners, she may raise a final clutch of eggs herself. In some places, the female is a faithful partner, sticking with one mate and helping him to raise their chicks.

A spotted sandpiper takes good care of its chicks.

Giant water bug

One **insect** father protects his eggs by himself. The giant water bug is an insect that lives in ponds and streams. After the male mates with the female, she deposits the eggs on the male's back. For the next few weeks, the father protects and cares for the eggs. It strokes them to keep them clean and makes sure they have enough oxygen—no small job for a water bug! When the eggs are ready to hatch, the father temporarily stops eating so he doesn't accidentally eat his newly hatched offspring.

The male giant water bug takes excellent care of the eggs on his back.

Several female rheas may lay eggs in the same ground nest, to be incubated by the male rhea.

Staying Close to Mom

Orangutans—a type of **ape**—are record-breaking mothers. They have a baby just once every seven to nine years. It is the longest gap between births of any creature. They care for their young for longer than any other animal parent (besides human beings). Orangutans live alone, so the female takes on all childcare duties. The newborn is born tiny and helpless, weighing just $3 \frac{1}{3}$ pounds (1.5 kilograms)—less than a human baby. The orangutan other nurses her offspring the entire time she is raising it—up to eight years!

Orangutans live high in the trees, so the mother has to make sure her baby does not fall. The newborn clings to its mother for the first four months and later holds her hand to swing through the trees. Even a two-year-old still needs help to pass safely from branch to branch, as it slowly learns to travel alone.

The youngsters have much more to learn from their mother. Orangutans are very smart animals, and mothers need a long time to pass on knowledge to their offspring. They teach them where to find tasty, edible fruits and how to tell when they are ripe. Mothers show their young how to build a nest of woven branches for resting and sleeping in the trees. A baby starts to practice these skills at six months old, but it takes three to four years to learn to build a sturdy treetop mattress.

A BABY ORANGUTAN is completely dependent on its mother for the first two years of its life.

Young orangutans seem to nurse more when there is not enough fruit to eat. In the wild, orangutans grow and develop slowly. Baby orangutans in zoos grow up more quickly because they have a plentiful food supply.

Youngsters stay with mom for six years or more, and by age 10, every orangutan has left home. Females stay in touch, visiting their mothers until they are about 15 or 16 years old, to maintain the family bond.

Hard-Working Moms (and Dads)

Glossary

amphibian a vertebrate with scaleless skin that usually lives part of its life in water and part on land. Vertebrate animals have a backbone.

antibody a substance that is used by the body to attack and neutralize harmful bacteria and viruses.

ape a member of a small group of mammals most like humans that includes chimpanzees, gorillas, gibbons, and orangutans. Unlike monkeys, apes do not have a tail.

brood a group of young animals that share the same parent or parents.

brood parasite an animal that relies on an animal of another species to raise its young.

carcass the dead body of an animal.

cocoon a covering made of soft threads spun by some insects as protection during the pupa stage, as they change into adults.

cold-blooded describes an animal that has little control over its body temperature.

colony a group of living things of one species that live together or grow in the same place.

egg a female sex cell, or the structure in which the embryo develops, usually outside the mother's body.

embryo an unborn or unhatched offspring.

extinct when every member of a species (kind) of living thing has died.

fertilize to join sperm from a male with egg from a female so that a young animal develops.

fry young fish, when newly hatched.

fungus (plural fungi) a living thing that usually grows on plants or on decaying matter. Yeast and mushrooms are fungi.

habitat the place where a living thing usually makes its home.

host a living thing that is either harmed or not affected in a symbiotic relationship. A symbiotic relationship is a relationship between two species from which at least one benefits.

incubate to keep fertilized eggs warm so that the embryos develop properly and hatch.

insect one of the major invertebrate groups. Invertebrate animals do not have a backbone. Insects have six legs and a three-part body.

larva (plural larvae) the active, immature stage of some animals, such as many insects, that is different from its adult form.

mammal one of the major vertebrate animal groups. Vertebrate animals have a backbone. Mammals feed their offspring on milk produced by the mother, and most have hair or fur.

marsupial one of the group of mammals that carry their young in a pocket of skin called a pouch.

mate the animal with which another animal partners to reproduce; the act of mating, when two animals come together to reproduce.

mimicry the action of copying something, or the close external resemblance of an animal to something else.

monotreme a group of mammals that now includes only the echidna and the platypus. They lay eggs, but also feed milk to their babies.

mucus a thick liquid that is produced in parts of animals' bodies.

nutrient a substance that is needed to keep a living thing alive and to help it grow.

ovary the organ in a female animal or plant that produces eggs or seeds.

predator an animal that hunts, kills, and eats other animals.

prey an animal that is hunted, killed, and eaten by another.

pupa (plural pupae) an insect in the stage of development between a larva and an adult insect.

regurgitate to bring food that has been swallowed back up into the mouth again.

reproduction the process by which living things produce their young, creating the next generation of their species, and passing on their genes.

reptile one of the major vertebrate animal groups. Vertebrate animals have a backbone. A reptile has dry, scaly skin and breathes air. Snakes, crocodiles, and lizards are all reptiles.

species a group of living things that have certain permanent traits in common and are able to reproduce with each other.

sperm a male sex cell.

suckle to feed a young animal with milk from the breast or teat. Only mammals suckle their young.

wean to gradually stop feeding a baby animal on its mother's milk.

BOOKS

All About Baby Zoo Animals series by Cecilia H. Brannon (Enslow Publishers 2016)

Baby Animals by Dorothea DePrisco (Animal Planet, 2017)

How Animals Build by Lonely Planet Kids (Lonely Planet, 2017)

Pocket Babies: And Other Amazing Marsupials by Sneed B. Collard III (Darby Creek Publishing, 2007)

WEBSITES

Discovery Kids
http://discoverykids.com
http://discoverykids.com/articles/five-fantastic-animal-fathers/
Many pages about animals, including an article about the best animal fathers.

Five animals you never knew make milk for their babies
http://www.bbc.co.uk/earth/story/20151016-five-animals-you-never-knew-make-milk-for-their-babies
Check out these nonmammals that nurse their young.

National Geographic Kids
http://www.natgeokids.com/uk/?s=animals
Pages about various animals.

Why are baby animals so cute?
http://www.bbc.co.uk/guides/zc8bgk7
This article explains why babies need to appeal to adults.

Index